PENGUIN HANDBOOKS

BASIC BALLET

W9-CAP-742

Joyce Mackie was born in 1920 and went to the City of London School. She started as a pupil at the Cone School of Dancing at the age of nine, and the Arts Educational School, as it is now called, was to command a large part of her life for more than forty years. She briefly performed as a dancer, but her main contribution to the dancing profession was as a teacher, and she was on the staff of the Arts Educational School for thirty-two years, during the latter part of which she was also head of vocational studies. Ms. Mackie's knowledge of dance covered a wide range of techniques, but she held a unique position in the ballet world; she had passed the advanced teachers' examination of the Royal Academy of Dancing and was a fellow of the Imperial Society Ballet Branch. Joyce Mackie died in 1978.

Basic

Joyce Mackie

Ballet

Penguin Books

PENGUIN BOOKS
Published by the Penguin Group
Penguin Books USA Inc.,
375 Hudson Street, New York, New York 10014, U.S.A.
Penguin Books Ltd, 27 Wrights Lane, London W8 5TZ, England
Penguin Books Australia Ltd, Ringwood, Victoria, Australia
Penguin Books Canada Ltd, 10 Alcorn Avenue,
Toronto, Ontario, Canada M4V 3B2
Penguin Books (N.Z.) Ltd, 182–190 Wairau Road, Auckland 10, New Zealand

Penguin Books Ltd, Registered Offices:
Harmondsworth, Middlesex, England

First published in Great Britain by W. Russell Turner 1978
First published in the United States of America by Penguin Books 1980

40 39 38 37 36 35

LIBRARY OF CONGRESS CATALOGING IN PUBLICATION DATA
Mackie, Joyce.
Basic ballet.
1. Ballet dancing.   I. Title.
GV1788.M25   1980   792.8'2   79–28212
ISBN 0 14 046.445 x

Copyright © W. Russell Turner, 1978
All rights reserved

Printed in the United States of America
Set in Janson

Contents

Foreword

Ballet dancing is a highly skilled theatrical art which has developed during the past four centuries from the dances performed at the courts of European royalty. This book is not intended to instruct in the technique of ballet—in fact it cannot be too strongly stressed that the lessons must be taken with a reputable teacher, otherwise untold harm can be done to young muscles, joints, and bones. However, children attending ballet classes will derive benefit from this book, since it will show them the full range of the technique and remind them of the correct basis of the exercises they are learning.

All children who learn ballet gain in grace and poise, even if they study for only a few years, since most children who attend classes have no intention of becoming professional. Although it is generally girls who study ballet, it can also be a help to boys, both athletically and nonathletically inclined. To the latter it can give exercise without the rough and tumble of the sports field, and to the former it can increase ability by its development of controlled movement, coordination, and self-discipline.

For anybody visiting the ballet, a knowledge and understanding of the subject must increase enjoyment and critical appreciation of the art, and this book tries to give an insight into what makes a dancer.

Beryl Grey
Artistic Director, The Festival Ballet

List of Illustrations

8

Allegro

Petit batterie

Grand batterie

This book shows all the basic movements in classical ballet, and they are arranged approximately in the sequence lessons usually follow.

Even the greatest dancers in the world practice the exercises and movements illustrated in this book. Pupils are always taken gradually through the various stages, and you should not try to tackle the difficult movements too soon.

The book is not intended as an instruction manual—it is essential that you take lessons from a properly qualified teacher—but it will help you to remember the exercises you have learned in class, and you can use it as a reference when practicing or visiting the ballet.

Exercises start at the *barre*, as this enables you to stretch your muscles and warm up while you are holding on to a support. Then, away from the *barre*, the same exercises are repeated, using various arm movements to gain balance. This is known as "center practice." After this come the slow sustained movements known as *"adage"*; then the turns, called "pirouettes." This is followed by small and big jumps known as *"allegro"*; and then beating the legs in the air, called *"batterie."* Finally, wearing *pointe* shoes, a girl will practice some of the earlier steps on full *pointe*, doing turns on the spot, and across and around the room.

Ballet as a theatrical art usually includes many other art forms in addition to the dancing, such as choreography, music, costume, scenery and lighting, but these are not dealt with in this book.

Many of the words used are French, and a list of the terms and their meaning is given on page 122.

Practice Dress

GIRLS

The usual practice dress for a ballet class consists of a simple tunic or leotard, with socks or tights and soft leather ballet shoes. Shoes must be bought to fit and not "to allow for growing." Ribbons should be sewn at each side of the shoe just behind the ankle bone. They should be tied neatly at the back and the ends tucked in.

The hair should be neat.

BOYS

The usual practice dress is a T-shirt, with black tights, white socks, and soft leather ballet shoes. These should be held on by elastic sewn onto the shoe just behind the ankle bone.

At the Barre

First you will learn to stand correctly at the *barre*. The *barre* is a smooth length of wood fixed to the wall at a height comfortable to hold without raising your shoulders.

Stand far enough from the *barre* for the hand to rest on it just in front of your body.

The weight of your body should be slightly forward over the balls of your feet, with your shoulders over your hips.

Most small children have "tum-

Fig. 1. Standing correctly at the *barre*.

mies," and they have to try very hard to brace these muscles so that the "seat" is relaxed down at the back and not "hitched up," so forcing out the rib cage.

Fig. 2. Foot positions

1st 2nd

Foot Positions

There are five positions of the feet, and all movements begin, end, or pass through one of these positions. In all positions the knees are straight and the legs are turned outward from the hips.

The weight is evenly placed on each foot.

1st position. Heels touch. The aim is to make a straight line with the feet, but this may not be possible at first.

2nd position. Heels about 12 inches apart, weight evenly on each foot.

3rd position. Feet are touching.

3rd   4th   5th   4th
opposite 1st   opposite 5th

Heel of right foot in front of hollow of left foot.

4th position opposite 1st. Right foot about 10 inches in front of left foot, with heels in line with each other.

4th position opposite 5th. Right foot about 10 inches in front of left foot with heel in line with toes.

5th position. Feet touching. Heel of right foot in front of left toe.

Fig. 3. Plié (in the 1st position)

Exercises at the Barre

THE PLIÉ

Bend your knees sideways over your toes and move back to your original position. The movement is practiced in all positions of the feet and should be as smooth as possible.

You should go down until your thighs are horizontal. Your heels

must be kept on the ground as long as possible (*demi plié*) and return again as soon as possible. In the 2nd and 4th open positions your heels remain down throughout.

Fig. 4.
Battement
tendu
(*en croix*)

BATTEMENT TENDU
Slide your foot along the floor
from the 5th position until fully
stretched in an open position (2nd
or 4th). Then slide it back to the
original position. The order of 4th
(5th) 2nd (5th) 4th is known as
en croix.

If your foot remains in the open position it is known as a *dégagé*.

The movement can also be started from 1st or 3rd position.

BATTEMENT GLISSÉ OR DÉGAGÉ

This movement is similar to a *battement tendu*, but it is done more sharply and your foot should leave the floor.

Fig. 5. Rond de jambe à terre
(en dehors)

ROND DE JAMBE À TERRE

This is an exercise to turn out your leg in the hip joint. Your body and supporting leg should remain quite still while your working leg moves in a circle, through 1st position, 4th front, 2nd position, 4th behind. The movement may be taken *en dehors* (away from your supporting leg) or *en dedans* (toward your supporting leg).

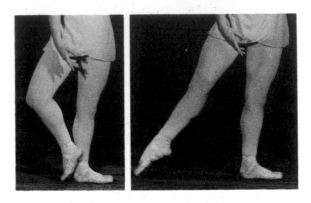

Fig. 6. Battement frappé

24

BATTEMENT FRAPPÉ

This is an exercise to strengthen your leg and foot.

Frappé means *"strike."*

Relax your foot on the ankle in front, then strike the floor with the ball of your foot and finish in 2nd position. Keeping your thigh still, bend the knee and bring your foot to the ankle behind.

Repeat the exercise, returning your foot to the original position.

Fig. 7. Petit battement sur le cou de pied.

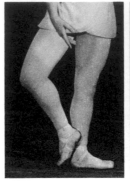

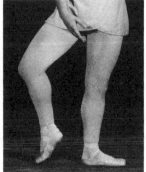

PETIT BATTEMENT SUR
LE COU DE PIED

This is an exercise to help *batterie* in the center, i.e., away from the *barre*.

Place your foot on the ankle (*le cou de pied*) as in *battement frappé*. Keeping your thigh still and moving from the knee, open the foot to a small 2nd, and return it to the ankle at the back.

Open again to a small 2nd and return to the front of your ankle.

Fig. 8. Battement fondu (devant)

BATTEMENT FONDU

This exercise helps you to achieve a soft and cushion-like landing, as if on a trampoline.

Stand with your foot in a *dégagé* 2nd and raise it to 45°. Smoothly bring your foot under the supporting knee, which should bend at the same time. Gradually straighten, opening your working leg to 4th or 2nd with a feeling of resistance.

Fig. 9.
Rond de jambe
en l'air
(*en dehors*)

ROND DE JAMBE EN L'AIR
For a single *ronde de jambe*, start
with your leg in 2nd position at
45° *en l'air* (see Fig. 8, 2nd photo).
Keeping the thigh still, trace your
foot through an elongated oval or
triangle, coming in just behind the
calf of your leg, passing to the

front and returning to 2nd position. This is known as *rond de jambe en dehors*. If the movement is reversed, i.e., coming to the front of the calf first, it is known as *en dedans*.

For a double *rond de jambe*, bring your foot in as for a single and open only halfway to 2nd position; come in again and finish in 2nd.

Fig. 10. Grand battement
(devant)

GRAND BATTEMENT

Your leg is "thrown" from 5th position to 4th or 2nd and returned to 5th. It passes through a *battement tendu* both on the way up and the way down.

BATTEMENT EN CLOCHE

Based on a *grand battement*, your leg swings from front to back passing through 1st position and should be the same height in front as behind.

Fig. 11. Developpé (*devant*)

DEVELOPPÉ

From 5th position, your foot is drawn up to the knee (*retiré;* see Fig. 11, 2nd photo) and extended to 4th devant, held there, and then closed again, with straight knees. The movement should be very smooth. Repeat this exercise *en croix.*

Fig. 12. Directions of the body

croisé devant   *en face*   *croisé derrière*

effacé
or *ouverte*

écarté

epaulé
or *ouverte derrière*

Center Practice

After completing practice of all the *barre* exercises, practice the same exercises in the center to develop stability. They can be done facing straight to the front (*en face*) or facing in different directions.

Fig. 13.
Arm
positions

En avant
5th en avant
1st position

À la seconde

Bras croise
4th en avant
3rd position

  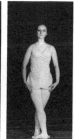  

Attitude
4th en haut
4th position

Attitude greque
4th crossed

Bras bas
5th en bas

Couronne
5th en haut
5th position

Demi bras
Demi seconde

Arm Positions

The different methods of training call the basic arm positions by different names.

Port de bras means "carriage of the arms." Your arms should move smoothly between the various positions, and at the same time you can transfer the weight from one foot to the other. At a later stage, your body also may be used in forward, backward, or side bends, or a circular movement incorporating all these.

39

Fig. 14. Coupé over

Adage

These are slow, sustained movements.

COUPÉ

This movement is used to change weight from one foot to the other.

Dégagé right foot 4th *devant* with a *demi plié* or *fondu* on the supporting leg. Draw foot back to left foot and rise on *demi pointe*.

Change weight, lowering right heel and placing left foot on *cou de pied*.

A "*coupé* over" is shown in Figure 14. When the movement is started with a *dégagé derrière*, it is known as "*coupé* under."

Fig. 15. Chassé (en avant)

CHASSÉ
This is a sliding movement of the foot forward, backward, or sideways.

Start in 5th position and *demi plié*. Keeping *demi plié*, slide your foot into open position.

To recover and finish the movement, transfer weight, *dégagé* foot, and close 5th.

Fig. 16. Arabesque

1st   *2nd*

ARABESQUE
This is a position on one leg with
the other extended behind—your
arms should make diagonal lines
with the palms turned down.

3rd

4th

5th

penchée

Fig. 17. *Attitude*

Fig. 18. *Grand rond de jambe (en dehors)*

ATTITUDE
This is a position on one leg with the other raised behind; the knee is bent so that the thigh is higher than the foot. The arms are usually in 4th position.

44

GRAND ROND DE JAMBE
(EN DEHORS)

Dèveloppé leg 4th *devant*. Carry your leg through 2nd round to 4th *derrière*. Close 5th position.

The movement is shown *en dehors*. It may also be taken *en dedans*, starting with *dèveloppé* 4th *derrière*, through 2nd round to 4th *devant*.

Fig. 19. Pirouette (*en dehors*)

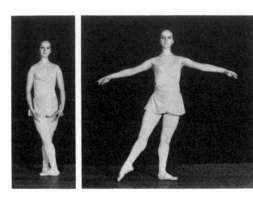

Pirouettes

These are turns on one leg with the other foot on the knee of the supporting leg. You can pirouette *en dehors* or *en dedans*.

En dehors. Prepare in 2nd, 4th, or 5th, with weight centrally be- tween both feet. Your right arm is in front, the left to the side. Open the right arm slightly and join the left to it; at the same time, raise your working foot and turn sharply toward it, rising on *demi pointe*.

47

Fig. 20. Pirouette (*en dedans*)

En dedans. Prepare in 4th with weight on your front foot and right arm across in front. Brush the back leg out to 2nd, opening your arms, then rise, bringing foot to knee, turning toward your supporting leg and joining the arms.

Fig. 21. Fouettés rond de jambe tournant

FOUETTÉS ROND DE JAMBE
EN TOURNANT

Usually known just as *fouettés*. The dancer makes a series of pirouettes remaining on one leg the whole time. Preparation is usually in 4th position as for pirouette *en dehors*—the dancer begins with a pirouette, lowers the supporting heel with *demi plié*, and extends the working leg to 4th *en l'air*, facing front. Continuing to turn, the dancer rises, whipping the working leg to 2nd position and again on to the knee. The arms follow the movement of the leg.

All these pirouettes call for quick turning, and the use of the head helps this. Keep your head to the front as long as possible, then turn it sharply to precede the body when facing front again.

All pirouettes and *fouettés rond de jambe* may be taken on the *pointe*.

Pirouettes can also be done in "open positions," such as 2nd *attitude* and *arabesque*. They are then done more slowly, with the flowing quality of *adage*.

Fig. 22. Sauté

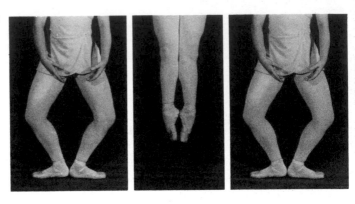

Allegro

This is the name given to small and big jumps.

SAUTÉ
Although the word means to jump, it is usually applied only to those jumps performed in 1st position.

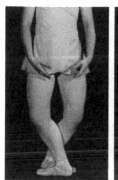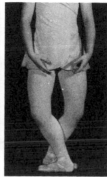

Fig. 23. Soubresaut

SOUBRESAUT
Spring in the air with your legs
well crossed in 5th position.

Fig. 24. Changement

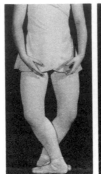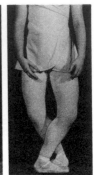

CHANGEMENT
Start in 5th position, spring into the air, change your legs, and land with the other foot in front.

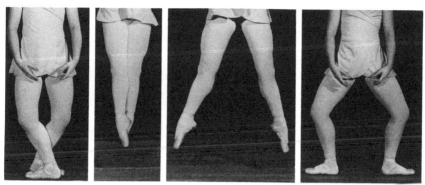

Fig. 25. Echappé

ECHAPPÉ
Start in 5th position, spring, and
land in either 4th or 2nd; spring
again and land in 5th.

Fig. 26. Temps levé

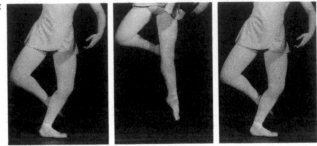

TEMPS LEVÉ
This is a spring or hop on one
foot. The other leg may be in any
position.

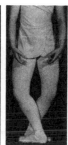

Fig. 27. Glissade devant

GLISSADE
This is started in 5th position and
demi plié. Dégagé the front foot
to 2nd; with a lilting movement,
transfer the weight and close the
other foot behind. This is a *glissade devant.* The movement can
also be performed *derrière* and
changé (changing feet).

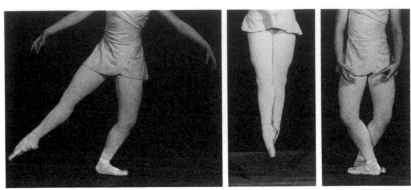

Fig. 28. Assemblé (devant)

ASSEMBLÉ

Demi plié in 5th position. *Dégagé* the front foot to 2nd, spring into the air, join the feet together in 5th, and alight. The movement can also be performed *derrière*, *dessus* (over), *dessous* (under), and traveling *en avant* and *en arrière* and *porté* (carried to the side).

Fig. 29. Jeté ordinaire

Jetés

A spring from one foot onto the other is called a *jeté* and there are many different types.

JETÉ ORDINAIRE
From the 5th position extend your left foot to 2nd, spring, and alight with left foot on the *cou de pied*. This may be done *derrière* and *devant*, as well as traveling *de côte* (sideways) and *en avant*, or *en arrière* with an extension to 4th.

59

Fig. 30. Jetés by half turns

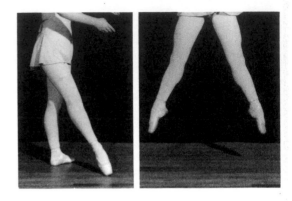

  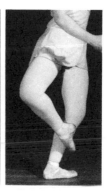

JETÉS BY HALF TURNS
These are based on *petits jetés* or
jetés ordinaires; taken diagonally,
the movement is usually *devant*.
The dancer always travels on the
first half turn, but not necessarily
on the second.

PETIT JETÉ (*Not illustrated*)
Raise your right foot onto the
cou de pied derrière, spring, and
alight on it with the left on the
cou de pied.

This step can also be done
devant.

Fig. 31. Jeté by full turn
(*saut de basque*)

JETÉ BY FULL TURN
(SAUT DE BASQUE)
With the right foot, *glissade devant* and step to the corner.

With a half turn, throw the left leg to 2nd and spring into the air,

taking both arms down and up to 5th (or *couronne*). Complete the turn and alight on left foot, with right foot under the knee. The step may be taken across the room, and in classical ballet it is often taken around the stage.

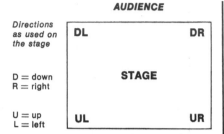

AUDIENCE

Directions as used on the stage

DL		DR
	STAGE	
UL		UR

D = down
R = right

U = up
L = left

BACK OF STAGE

Stage Directions

Fig. 32. Grand jeté en tournant

GRAND JETÉ EN TOURNANT
Commence down right in 2nd *arabesque à terre* on right foot. With a running movement, step back on left foot, then across and toward up left corner with right foot forward toward up left cor-

ner. With left foot (*pas de boureé*) brush right leg forward and spring into the air, taking arms down and up to 5th position (or *couronne*). Leaving right leg in the air, make a half turn to the left, change the legs at the back, and land on the right foot with left leg extended behind and arms open in *demi bras*.

Fig. 33.
Jeté
en avant

JETÉ EN AVANT
Brush the right leg forward, then leap up and forward through the air, landing on right foot with left leg extended behind. This is usu-ally preceded by two or three running steps.

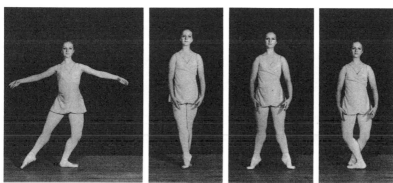

Fig. 34. Pas de bourrée (devant)

PAS DE BOURRÉE

Dégagé right foot to 2nd with *fondu* on left. Draw legs together rising on *demi pointe*. Step left to 2nd, remaining on *demi pointe*, close right foot in 5th on *demi plié*. The step can be taken *devant*, *derrière*, over and under, and turning.

Fig. 35. Open *pas de bourrée*

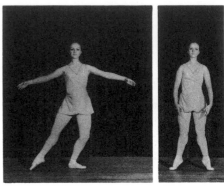

alternative ending

OPEN PAS DE BOURRÉE

Dégagé right foot to 2nd, then step onto it on *demi pointe;* join left foot in 5th, lower the supporting heel, and either *dégagé* right foot to 2nd, or alternatively, place weight on it, showing *demi plié* in 2nd. The movement can also be taken *en avant* and *en arrière,* using 4th position.

Fig. 36. Pas de chat

PAS DE CHAT

Stand in 5th position with your right foot behind. Raise your right foot with knee bent, spring into the air while bending up left leg, land on your right foot, and close left foot in 5th *devant*.

GARGOUILLADE (*Not illustrated*)
Stand in 5th position with right foot front. Raise right foot as in *pas de chat* and open it slightly to side, then spring into the air making a small double *rond de jambe en l'air en dehors*. Finish as for a *pas de chat*, closing left foot in front. The second leg may make a *rond de jambe en dedans* before closing. The whole step may be started with the back foot and performed *en dedans;* then it does not change feet.

71

Fig. 37. Sissone ordinaire
(devant)

Sissones

A sissone is a spring off two feet landing on one.

SISSONE ORDINAIRE
Spring from 5th position and alight raising one foot under the knee. The step is performed *devant, derrière passé,* and *en tournant.*

Fig. 38. Sissone
ouverte
(*en avant*)

SISSONE OUVERTE

Spring from 5th and alight with one leg extended. The step is taken *en avant*, *en arrière*, and *de côté*.

SISSONE FERMÉE

As *ouverte*, but immediately after alighting, close in 5th position.

SISSONE DOUBLÉE

Consists of *sissone ouverte de côté*, a *coupé*, and an *assemblé*.

73

Fig. 39. Balloné
(*devant*)

BALLONÉ (DEVANT)
Stand on your left foot, with the right foot under the knee, then *temps levé* traveling forward, at the same time extending your right leg. Alight and bring the right foot under the knee again. The step is also taken *en arrière* and *de côté*.

BALLONÉ COMPOSÉ
Perform a simple *balloné* (as above) but immediately extend the working leg again; step forward, *dégagé derrière*, and close 5th.

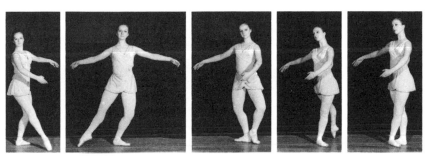

Fig. 40. Pas de basque (glissé)

PAS DE BASQUE (GLISSÉ)

Demi plié with your right foot in front, make half a *rond de jambe* to 2nd.

Take weight onto the right foot, *chassé* through with the left foot, *dégagé* right foot *derrière,* and close to 5th.

The step can also be performed with a spring (*sauté*) or with straight legs (*grand pas de basque*). All can be taken *en arrière*.

Fig. 41. Ballotté

BALLOTTÉ

Stand on your left foot, with right foot *dégagé derrière*. Spring and join both feet under your body, alighting on your right foot with left leg extended.

Spring and join feet again.

Alight on your left foot with right leg extended. This step is danced by Giselle and Albrecht in the first act of the ballet *Giselle*.

Fig. 42. *Demi contretemps*

DEMI CONTRETEMPS
This consists of a *temps levé* and
a *chassé passé*.

Fig. 13. Full *contretemps*

FULL CONTRETEMPS
This consists of a *coupé* under,
chassé en avant, and a *demi contretemps*.

Fig. 44. Fouetté

FOUETTÉ

This is a movement starting in 4th position, passing through 2nd position, and finishing in arabesque.

Relevé on your left leg, brushing the right leg through 4th to 2nd *en l'air*. Turn in the air to *arabesque* and land in this position. It is often preceded either by a *demi contretemps*, or a *pas de bourrée*, as in *grand jeté en tournant*. The movement may be done by a spring instead of a *relevé*.

Fig. 45. Tour en l'air

TOUR EN L'AIR

This movement is performed by
male dancers; the step consists of
a *changement* turning toward the
front foot, either once or twice in
the air.

Fig. 46. Changement battu

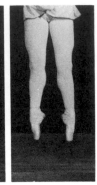

Petit Batterie

This consists of the small steps of *allegro* performed with a beat at the base of the calf before landing.

CHANGEMENT BATTU
Stand in 5th position and *demi plié*. Spring into the air, slightly parting the legs, beat them at the base of the calf, and land with the other foot in front.

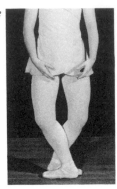

Fig. 48. Entrechat quatre

Fig. 47. Entrechat trois

ENTRECHAT TROIS
If the *changement battu* finishes
on one foot, it is known as an
entrechat trois.

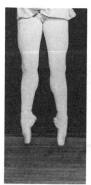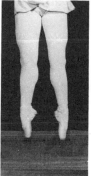

ENTRECHAT QUATRE

Stand in 5th position and *demi plié* as for *changement battu*. Spring into the air and change the legs before beating and then change again before alighting. If the step finishes on one foot, it is known as an *entrechat cinq*.

Fig. 49. Echappé battu

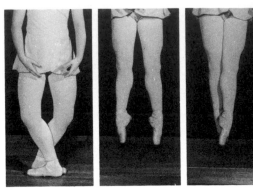

ECHAPPÉ BATTU
Taken to 2nd position. The beat to
2nd is that of *entrechat quatre*.
Beat to 5th position may be either
an *entrechat* or a *changement
battu*.

Fig. 50. Brisé (over or *dessus*)

BRISÉ

Stand 5th position, right foot front, *demi plié*. *Dégagé* left foot to 2nd, then spring into the air, bringing the right leg up underneath the left to make the beat. Change legs again and finish right foot front.

Figure 50 shows a *brisé* over. It can also be performed under, *devant, derrière, en avant,* or *en arrière*. It may also be started or finished on one foot.

JETÉ, ASSEMBLÉ, AND
PAS DE BASQUE
All these basic steps may be performed with the beat of a *changement battu*.

SISSONE BATTU
En avant and *en arrière* are performed with the beat of an *entrechat quatre*. *De côté* with the beat of either an *entrechat* or a *changement*, but more usually the former.

Grand Batterie

This uses more elevation than *petit batterie*, and the legs are more fully crossed.

ENTRECHAT SIX
An *entrechat quatre* with an extra beat, therefore calling for more elevation.

ENTRECHAT SIX DE CÔTÉ
A *brisé* over with an extra beat, therefore calling for more elevation. The step is usually preceded by a *glissade* or a *demi contretemps*.

Fig. 51. Brisé volé

BRISÉ VOLÉ

Begin right foot *dégagé* 4th *derrière*. Brush the leg through 1st position on a *demi plié*, spring, and perform a *jeté battu devant* with straight legs. Brush the left leg back through 1st position and

perform a *jeté battu derrière* with straight legs.

On the first part of the step the body tilts forward over the legs, and on the second tilts backward —the arms may be used as wings to give the effect of flying. This step may be seen in the Bluebird variation from the last act of *Sleeping Beauty*.

Fig. 52. Cabriole devant

CABRIOLE DEVANT

Stand with right foot *dégagé* 4th *derrière*. Brush the right leg through 1st to 4th *en l'air*, then spring into the air and beat the left leg up underneath the right leg. Alight on left foot with a *grand battement* of the right leg. Close 5th. This step is usually preceded by a *demi contretemps* or a *glissade derrière*. The step can also be performed *derrière* or *de côté*.

FOUETTÉ BATTU

This is a *demi contretemps fouetté sauté*, performed with the

beat of an open *cabriole devant*, and landing in *arabesque*.

The step can also be performed *en tournant* preceded by a *pas de bourrée*. The beat may be *devant* followed by the turn, or the turn may come first followed by a beat *derrière*.

GRAND JETÉ BATTU

This consists of a *pas de bourrée grand jeté en tournant*, with *jeté battu derrière* after the turn and before alighting.

Pointe Work

Pointe work should not be attempted until the bones have ossified (hardened); otherwise malformation of the feet may occur. It is also essential that the muscles in the pupil's back and legs are strong enough to enable the movements to be performed without strain and maintaining a correct stance. All steps should first of all be practiced on the *demi pointe*.

ECHAPPÉ
Start *demi plié* in 5th position. With a very slight spring, open the legs to 2nd and alight on full *pointe;* then, with a slight spring, return to 5th position. This can also be performed to 4th position.

RELEVÉ
Relevé may be taken on two feet in any of the five positions. *Demi plié* and, with a slight spring, draw

the legs under the body so that the toe takes the place of the heel. Then, with a slight spring, return to original position.

This movement is also performed drawing the supporting leg under the body, as previously explained, and raising the working foot to the knee and returning to 5th position; it can be taken *devant*, *derrière*, and *passé*.

Thirdly, it can also be taken remaining on one leg. The supporting leg is again drawn under the body, while the working leg is either extended to an open position and returned to a position under the knee, or held throughout in one position, such as an *arabesque*.

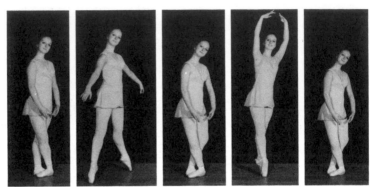

Fig. 53. Enchainement of echappé 2nd, relevé 5th, relevé devant,

and *relevé en avant*

ENCHAINEMENT
An *enchainement* consists of two
or more steps joined together.

Fig. 54. Demi detourné

DEMI DETOURNÉ
Relevé in 5th, make a half turn toward back foot, and lower with the other foot in front.

Fig. 55. Full *detourné*

FULL DETOURNÉ
Relevé in 5th, but make a complete turn before lowering, with other foot in front.

Fig. 56.
Enchainement
of *posé* turns
and *posés*

posé developpé   *posé arabesque*

POSÉ

A *posé* is a step in any direction and in any position. The most common *posés* are: *posé coupé*, with the foot placed under the knee; *posé developpé*, with the foot passing through *retiré;* and *posé arabesque*. The name is also given to a step on the flat of the foot, preceding a *temps levé*.

posé turn *coupé*   lame duck

POSÉ TURNS

These are based on *posé coupé*, but turning on the *posé*. This may be taken across or around the stage (*manége*) and performed *en dedans* or *en dehors*. When per-formed *en dehors*, they are often known as "lame ducks."

Fig. 57. Petit pas de basque en tournant

PETIT PAS DE BASQUE
EN TOURNANT

This is a step taken across or around the stage. Spring onto right foot on *pointe*, starting to turn to right, sharply close left foot into 5th, *demi detourné*, and lower immediately, releasing right foot.

Fig. 58. Chaînes or petits tours

CHAÎNES OR PETITS TOURS
The feet should be kept in 1st position and a half turn made on each step across the stage. The arms are held just in front of the body, and the turns are taken as quickly as possible.

Fig. 59. Pas de
bourrée pique

PAS DE BOURRÉE COURU
This is a series of little running
steps in 5th position—the knees are
slightly relaxed and the back leg
should move first, so that a good
5th position is maintained. The
steps should be quick, and the
whole movement travels as much
as possible, using a varied *port de
bras*.

PAS DE BOURRÉE PIQUE
Similar to that explained in *Allegro*
section (see page 68), but the feet
are picked up to the knee.

Fig. 60.
Rond de jambe relevé

ROND DE JAMBE RELEVÉ
Stand in 5th, right foot behind.
Relevé on left foot with right leg
in 2nd, single or double *rond de jambe*, and close right foot front.
The step is often preceded by a
glissade and may also be taken
sauté.

FOUETTÉ RELEVÉ
As taken in *Allegro* section (see
page 80).

developpé à la seconde   *developpé attitude devant*

Double Work

The highlight of all classical ballets is the *grand pas de deux*, performed by the ballerina and her cavalier. This consists of an *entrée*, a supported *adage*, solos for the dancers, and a coda, in which excitement is built up with jumps and beats from the man and turns from the girl.

The following section deals with the supported *adage*.

It is essential that the girl should be so well placed that she needs little support from her part-

Fig. 61. Enchainement

fouetté to *attitude derrière*

promenade finishing in *arabesque penchée*

ner—he is not there for her to lean on!

For his part, the "cavalier" must remember that his first duty is to show off the ballerina, and that when holding her he must avoid digging his fingers into her. The hands are therefore held as flat as possible, with the fingers in front of the body and the thumb behind. He also has to judge how close to the girl he must stand to keep her on balance.

111

Fig. 62. Pirouette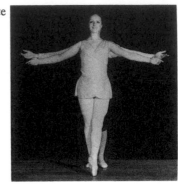

PIROUETTE

For the preparation, the girl does a little *couru* forward and lowers into a *demi plié* in 4th—the boy's hands are lightly on her waist. When she turns, her arms are crossed on her chest with the elbows down, so that there is no chance of her hitting her partner. The boy uses his right hand to help give extra impetus to the right; the girl turns inside his left arm; then he uses his right hand to control the end of the pirouette.

Fig. 63. Fouetté rond de jambe en tournant finishing in arabesque

FOUETTÉ ROND DE JAMBE
EN TOURNANT

The girl stands on *pointe* in 5th position; the fingers of her raised arm are curled around the index finger of the boy; her hand is holding his out in 2nd position. She makes a *developpé* 4th *devant*

with the right leg, pressing with her left hand to give extra impetus, then a *fouetté en tournant* with the left hand across her chest. At the end of the turn she takes the boy's left hand again. As long as the girl holds her back firm, the boy can help her to increase the number of the turns performed.

Fig. 64. Shoulder lift

SHOULDER LIFT

The simplest lift is onto the shoulder. The preparation is an *assemblé* during which the boy bends his knees to get his body under the girl. Then using first his body weight and then his arms, he lifts the girl up and back over the right shoulder and seats her on it. The girl must lift herself as much as possible, and then bends her left knee up with the right leg over it in *attitude devant*.

Arabesque   pirouette

Fig. 65.
This series of
movements is seen in
many classical ballets

fish dive

FISH DIVE
A position in which the boy
lunges and the girl takes an *arabesque penchée*, with the underneath leg bent and the top one
straight.

Fig. 66. Bluebird lift

BLUEBIRD LIFT

The girl makes a *pas de bourrée grand jeté en tournant;* as she steps, the boy kneels and places his right shoulder under her body, and as she jumps he rises up. This lift is seen in the Bluebird *pas de deux* from *Sleeping Beauty.*

It will be seen from these descriptions that complete coordination and sympathy between the partners are essential and are gained only with time and practice.

Some French Terms Used in Ballet

Adage—A slow, carefully controlled type of movement.

en l'air—In the air.

Allegro—A cheerful, brisk type of movement.

Arabesque—A Moorish design. A pose in which the dancer stands on one leg with the other raised behind.

en arrière—Backwards.

Assemblé—To join together. A leap in the air, bringing feet together before alighting.

Attitude—A standing position (see page 00).

en avant—Forward.

Balloné—A bouncing step. With one foot raised to the other knee, the dancer springs up, straightening and bending raised leg.

Ballotté—To toss. The dancer springs on one foot, tossing the other leg in the air.

Bas—Down.

Batterie—A jump where the dancer beats the calves together.

Battement—A beating movement.

Battu—Beaten.

Bras—Arm.

Brisé—To break. The dancer jumps from one foot, beats legs together and lands on both feet.

Cabriole—To caper. A step where one leg is beaten against the other in mid air.

Changé, changement — Changing the position of the feet.

Chassé—A sliding step.

Chaînes—A series of small turning steps.

Cinque—Five.

Cloche—Bell.

Contretemps—In syncopation or against the time.

de côté—Sideways.

Cou de pied—Ankle joint.

Coupé—Cut.

en couronne—A crown. Where the arms are held in a curve above the head.

Couru—Running.

Croisé—Crossed. Where the dancer's body is placed obliquely toward the audience.

en dedans—Inwards.

Dégagé—To disengage the foot from a closed to an open position.

en dehors—Outwards.

Demi—Half.

Derrière—Behind.

Dessous—Under.

Dessus—Over.

Detourné—Turned away.

Deux—Two.

Devant—In front.

Developpé—An unfolding of the leg.

Ecarté—Separated.

Echappé—An escaping of the feet from each other.

Effacé—Where the dancer's body is placed obliquely from the audience.

Elancé—To dart.

Entrechat (from the Italian *intrecciare*—to weave)—A vertical jump where the calves beat together and feet change position.

Epaulé, epaulement—The shoulders are turned at an angle to the hips.

Fondu—Melting. A *plié* on one leg.

Fouetté—To whip.

Frappé—To strike.

Gargouillade—A gurgle.

Glissé—To slide, allowing foot to leave the floor.

Glissade—A slow, sliding step.

Grand—Big.

Greque—Greek.

en haut—Up.

Jambe—Leg.

Jeté—Thrown. The basic jump from one leg to the other, the first leg usually being "thrown."

Levé—Lifted.

en manège—Traveling right around the stage.

Ouverte—Open.

Pas de basque—A step of the Basque country. A circular swaying movement.

Pas de bourrée—To hustle. A step where the weight is transferred quickly from one foot to the other.

Pas de chat—A catlike step.

Petit—Small.

Penché—To tilt. On one leg with the other leg raised.

Pied—Foot.

Plié Bend—A bending of the knees over the toes.

Pique—To prick. A sharp movement of the foot.

Porté—Carried. A movement carried through the air, usually to the side.

Port de bras—Graceful carriage of the arms.

Posé—To place. A step.

Quatre—Four.

Relevé—To rise up on the toes.

Retiré—The drawing up of one foot to touch the other leg with pointed toe.

Rond de jambe—Circling the leg.

Saut, sauté—A simple jump.

Seconde—Second.

Sissone—A simple step of elevation.

Soubresaut—A jump with the feet in 5th position.

Temps levé—A small jump where weight is not transferred.